THE REMINISCENCES OF
Mr. John F. Dille Jr.

INTERVIEWED BY

Paul Stillwell

U.S. Naval Institute • Annapolis, Maryland

Copyright © 2014

JOHN FLINT DILLE JR

John Flint Dille Jr., was a newspaper and broadcasting executive. For years he was the owner, publisher and editor of *The Elkhart Truth* in Elkhart, Indiana.

Mr. Dille's father was originally an educator – he founded Dixon College in Illinois, alma mater of Ronald Reagan. Mr. Dille Sr., eventually gravitated to the University of Chicago and became fascinated with the newspaper syndicate business. He founded the National Newspaper Syndicate, which sold features such as comics, packaged editorials and news features to newspapers around the world. He personally developed "Buck Rogers" in the 1920s, a comic strip that proved to be mightily prophetic and whose copyright served the Dille family well for many years.

John F. Dille Jr., after receiving his degree from the University of Chicago, went on the road selling national newspaper syndicate products at the request of his father. Mr. Dille found Elkhart, Indiana, on his list of towns harboring newspapers to which he could "pitch" comic strips and other features – such as the Sam Snead golf column.

Coincidentally, Mr. Dille also found a University of Chicago fraternity brother whose family owned a portion of *The Elkhart Truth*. That chap asked Mr. Dille one day if he knew of anybody whom he might recommend to become publisher of *The Truth* as Tom Keene, the publisher at the time, was about to retire. Mr. Dille lined up several candidates – but *The Truth* folk had grown to like Mr. Dille so well that eventually the job was offered to him. In 1952 Mr. Dille left the National Newspaper Syndicate in Chicago to come to the wilds – by his reckoning – of Elkhart, Indiana. The newspaper at that time was owned by the Greenleaf and Beardsley families.

Through the years the Greenleaf and Beardsley families provided Mr. Dille with the opportunity of purchasing *The Truth*. Eventually he became the sole owner, and also became involved with radio and television acquisitions in Elkhart, South Bend, and Fort Wayne.

Mr. Dille returned to the University of Chicago in the mid-50s and earned a Masters degree in mass media/communications. Throughout his career he was a recipient of numerous honorary degrees and awards, including the Minnesota award for Distinguished Service in Journalism in 1977. He was also vice-chairman of the Indiana Toll Road Commission, president of the Chief Executives Forum, the Elkhart Chamber of Commerce and served as a director emeritus of Society (now Key) Bank. He was president of the ABC network television affiliates and chairman of the National Association of Broadcasters.

Mr. Dille also was on the board of the Beardsley Foundation for many years and was a great supporter of Ruthmere.

Among the many achievements of his long and distinguished career, Mr. Dille probably was most proud of his service as a U.S. Navy officer during World War II – during which he was a key officer in the training of the first group of Black line officers commissioned for Naval service. The thirteen men were commissioned as a group and they and Dille remained friends throughout their lives.

Mr. Dille, who was born 14 November 1913 in Chicago, passed away on 7 October 1994 in Elkhart at the age of 80.

Obituaries

JOHN F. DILLE JR.

ELKHART — Friends of John Flint Dille, Jr., 80, of 1 Holly Lane, may call from 3 to 5 and 7 to 9 p.m. Monday at Hartzler-Gutermuth Funeral Home. Funeral services will be at 11 a.m. Tuesday at St. John's Episcopal Church. The Rev. George Minnix, Chaplain Emeritus of Howe Military Academy, will officiate. The body will be cremated with entombment in the columbarium at Rice Cemetery.

Mr. Dille, broadcasting executive and owner and editor of *The Elkhart Truth* died Friday afternoon (Oct. 7, 1994) at his residence of an apparent heart attack.

He was born Nov. 14, 1913, in Chicago. He married Jayne Paulman on April 9, 1938, in Chicago. She survives with one daughter, Joanne Barrett of Atlanta, Ga.; one son, John Flint Dille III of Elkhart; and five grandchildren. One brother, Robert C. Dille, preceded him in death.

At the time of his death, he was chairman of the board of Truth Publishing Company and Pathfinder Communications Corp. The companies publish *The Truth* and the Greencastle Banner Graphic newspapers and operate radio stations in Elkhart, Fort Wayne, Grand Rapids, Mich., Cincinnati, Ohio and Tulsa, Okla.

Mr. Dille came to *The Truth* June 1, 1952, as editor, publisher and vice president of Truth Publishing Company. At that time, the company owned and operated the newspaper and WTRC radio, the local NBC affiliate.

He received his undergraduate degree from the University of Chicago in 1935 and then joined the National Newspaper Service syndicate, which was founded and headed by his father, John Flint Dille.

During World War II, Dille was ordered to active duty with the U.S. Navy as a lieutenant and was a key officer in the training of the first black line officers in the Navy.

Mr. Dille was elected to the American Society of Newspaper Editors and served as chairman of the National Association of Broadcasters. He returned to school in Chicago in the mid-50s to earn a master's degree in mass-media communications. He also received a number of honorary degrees and awards, including the Minnesota Award for Distinguished Service in Journalism in 1977. He served as chairman of the Minority Broadcaster Investment Fund and vice president of Broadcast Pioneers. In addition, he served as vice chairman of the Indiana Toll Road Commission, was a past president of the Chief Executives Forum and the Elkhart Chamber of Commerce and was director emeritus of Society Bank. He served on the board of the Beardsley Foundation for many years. He also was a member of Elcona Country Club, Congressional Country Club, National Press Club and International Club.

Memorial contributions may be made to Diabetic Research at the University of Chicago.

Authorization

The U.S. Naval Institute is hereby authorized to make available to individuals, libraries, and other repositories of its choosing the transcripts of two oral history interviews concerning the life and career of the undersigned. The interviews were recorded on 7 October 1986 and 25 August 1989 in collaboration with Paul Stillwell for the U.S. Naval Institute.

The undersigned does hereby release and assign to the U.S. Naval Institute all right, title, restrictions, and interest in the interviews. The copyright in both the oral and transcribed versions shall be the sole property of the U.S. Naval Institute. The tape recordings of the interviews are and will remain the property of the U.S. Naval Institute.

Signed and sealed this 29th day of November 1993.

John F. Dille, Jr.

Interview Number 1 with Mr. John F. Dille Jr.

Place: Mr. Dille's office at Federated Media, Elkhart, Indiana

Date: Tuesday, 7 October 1986

Interviewer: Paul Stillwell

Paul Stillwell: Mr. Dille, I really appreciate your being able to see me on this, because this will add another dimension to our discussion of the Golden Thirteen and the early years of the black naval officers with the U.S. Navy. In order to provide some background, could you give me, please, a brief biographical sketch on yourself before you got into the Navy?

Mr. Dille: I'm grateful for your being interested in coming down here from Chicago and talking to me about this.

I was born in Chicago, as a matter of fact, on Belmont Avenue, in an apartment one block from Sheridan Road, which then literally was a lake before the land was built out farther. Sometime later, my primary grades in school, we moved to Evanston, and I really grew up in Evanston. I went to Evanston High School and from there to the University of Chicago. I have two degrees from the University of Chicago. I met the girl who became my wife, also a graduate of the University of Chicago, there. We lived in the Chicago area.

I was in the newspaper feature syndication business from the time I finished school until I had an opportunity to buy an interest in the daily newspaper in Elkhart, Indiana. That was a very appealing idea, so I acted upon it. In 1952, I moved to Elkhart and took over the responsibility for the operation of the daily newspaper, and it had an AM radio station at that time.[*] As the years have gone by, we built the organization considerably. My son is actually the head of it now.[†]

---

[*] The newspaper is named *The Elkhart Truth*.
[†] The son is John F. Dille III

We're operating two daily newspapers, the other one being in Greencastle, Indiana. Interestingly, Greencastle is the home and birthplace of Sigma Delta Chi, the journalistic fraternity.

Paul Stillwell: And Depauw University.

Mr. Dille: And Depauw University. He has also added two radio stations, an AM and FM, adjacent to Tulsa, Oklahoma, to increase our group to a total of ten; that is, five AM-FM combinations in five markets, South Bend-Elkhart being the original home market, and subsequently Fort Wayne, Grand Rapids, Cincinnati, and now Tulsa. I don't know to what extent you want to carry the biographical information, since we're talking about the Navy.

Paul Stillwell: I'd be interested in what you were doing in the years just prior to World War II.

Mr. Dille: I was in the newspaper features syndication business.

Paul Stillwell: With what organization?

Mr. Dille: The name was National Newspaper Service. It was not identified with any of the newspaper chains, as a number of the syndicates were. It was an independent which my father had started.* It handled some very well known newspaper features at that time, the features being the editorial content of the newspaper—as distinguished from any advertising, but not news. These features included columns, comic strips, panels, cartoons, articles, that sort of thing.

Paul Stillwell: Did you as an individual have a particular specialty within the syndicate?

---

* John F. Dille Sr. was president of the National Newspaper Service. In 1929 he created a comic strip titled "Buck Rogers in the 25th Century." It featured interplanetary warfare and communications and employed imaginary weapons such as death rays and rocket pistols. Dille developed the concept for the strip and supplied story ideas; the artist was Richard Calkins. To this day the name "Buck Rogers" is still linked with futuristic ideas.

Mr. Dille: No. I started, of course, as a trainee and wound up in administration. I did do a lot of editing of newspaper columns for accuracy and for policy and for tastefulness, that kind of thing. I did develop one amusing feature of my own, which I syndicated. Actually, they were puzzles, but they were called Brain Twizzlers by Professor—I appropriated that title—J D. Flint, Flint being my middle name. It proved to be a quite successful, amusing, entertaining feature and ran in a substantial number of outstanding American newspapers.

In the process of working with the features syndicate, I traveled the country a great deal: selling features, calling upon newspapers, on managing editors and publishers, to try to persuade them to buy more of National Newspaper Service's features.

I had become married, and we had a son born in August of 1941. When the Japanese bombed Pearl Harbor four months later, I had a decision to make in terms of my own position. It's been traditional in our family to serve if needed. We've had a number of military men in our past generations. I was free of any obligation in terms of the government's decision—the draft law and that kind of thing—because I was married and had a child. I was classified Class III—I believe they called it at that time—with very little likelihood of my being called to active duty. But I felt that it was a situation where I would feel better in my own sense of obligation by volunteering for service.

I applied for a direct commission in the United States Navy. I had had years of military training in high school and university through the ROTC training route.[*] The Navy granted me a commission directly and ordered me to Great Lakes Naval Training Station.[†]

Paul Stillwell: Why did you seek the Navy rather than one of the other services?

Mr. Dille: Partly, I guess, because I'm something of a germophobe, and I'm very, very high on hygiene and cleanliness. To me, the Army meant visions of crawling through the

---

[*] ROTC – Reserve officer training corps.
[†] Great Lakes, Illinois, a town on the shore of Lake Michigan, about 30 miles north of downtown Chicago, was the site of a large naval training station that included recruit training and a number of specialized schools.

mud on your stomach while cradling your rifle—bayoneted rifle—in your elbows. That vision did not appeal to me at all. Being by that time in my late 20s—I was born in 1913—I thought it was a little late to start to learn to become an aviator. Also, being over 6 feet, 3 inches tall and wearing size 13 shoes, I felt that the typical airplane cockpit and I would not be a very comfortable match.

Paul Stillwell: Had you had any training or precept from your parents about race relations prior to the time you got out on your own? What was your family indoctrination in that?

Mr. Dille: I do not think my family had any particular description of their own attitudes, other than they were certainly good Christian individuals. Evanston was—certainly in those years, and perhaps still is—a very hospitable community toward minority individuals, notably blacks. As a matter of fact, I think I'm correct in saying that Evanston was one of the northern terminals for the so-called underground railway in the days when slavery was being broken up. So I grew up in a community and in a public high school with numerous minority friends and had no feeling of discrimination.

Paul Stillwell: What do you remember of your early experiences in the Navy?

Mr. Dille: Since I'd had so much military training, I was ordered to the recruit training division at Great Lakes. Then, after a short period of indoctrination, I was put in command of a battalion of approximately 500 or 600 recruits. These were new men in the Navy receiving their initial so-called boot camp training. That was my first assignment with the Navy.

Paul Stillwell: You were probably learning a good deal right along with the boots, since you were new to the Navy also.

Mr. Dille: Well, yes, but only in the sense of those terms and those activities that are peculiar to the Navy. The basic military is pretty standard, and I'd had a lot of that, so it was a quite easy adaptation for me. Boot training is largely marching the men around.

Paul Stillwell: And very elementary studies.

Mr. Dille: Very elementary studies and not highly Navy in any presentations.

Paul Stillwell: Was it essentially your administrative skills that were being called on as a recruit training battalion commander?

Mr. Dille: I don't think particularly so. I think it was a matter of drawing on my own military background and knowledge of military protocol, military courtesy, fundamental individual military maneuvers, and the structural organization of battalions, platoons, squads, and so on, and the ability to command. Now, whether you'd classify these all together as administrative, I am not so sure. It required administration in the sense of evaluating disciplinary problems and decisions on how to mete out disciplinary actions, because, of course, in any group of hundreds of men, you're going to have some recalcitrants who will go over the edge and break the rules.

Paul Stillwell: Did you get into contact with the recruits a good bit, conducting inspections, making speeches to them, and so forth?

Mr. Dille: Yes. Yes. In terms of inspections, of course, it's traditional in the Navy for the commanding officer or captain, if you will, to inspect his command. If it's at sea, the captain, in most cases, personally prefers to. He, of course, may delegate the responsibility to a chief of staff or some other officer. But frequently it's the captain himself who wants to go around the ship or the building, whatever the command is, to see whether or not it is being operated in the fashion for which he is held responsible by higher authority and in the fashion for which he holds those under him responsible for maintaining.

Paul Stillwell: It was a convenient assignment, relatively close to home. Did you seek a sea assignment at all?

Mr. Dille: No, I did not seek a sea assignment. It certainly was very conveniently close to home. As a matter of fact, I think my commuting from my home, then in Highland Park, to Great Lakes took less time than commuting to my office in downtown Chicago.

Paul Stillwell: Did you have a desire to get out and get into the action?

Mr. Dille: During my physical examination by the Navy, I had all the qualifications and passed all of the tests required. In terms of the physical examination, the Navy determined that I was at least partially defective in color perception. That came to be an interesting joke later on. A Japanese scientist named Ishihara had invented a test to determine qualifications for that capacity. Curiously, the U.S. Navy at that time was using that test for its naval officers, even in the wake of the Japanese bombing of Pearl Harbor. For the reason that the Navy wasn't sure that I would read signal flags correctly, it tended not to give me any sea assignments, and that was perfectly all right with me. Actually, I can tell any shade. For example, take pink and green. I can go down many shades of pink and green and identify them to an interior decorator's satisfaction, but the Navy doesn't take any chances.

Paul Stillwell: I'm curious why you went into this kind of a command assignment rather than something in the public information field.

Mr. Dille: That was determined, really, by the Navy. Later on, I did wind up in the public information service in the Pacific. But initially, their need for my skills in training men was greater than the need for men with newspaper and journalism abilities.

Paul Stillwell: You were in a training billet. Did you have any background in that area?

Mr. Dille: Yes, my own military training was ideally adapted, because new recruits had to be formed into marching units, if for no other reason than to move them from one place to another. In the process, of course, it was desirable to have them learn it properly, learn it at the correct pace, the correct rhythm, and with the correct attention to good military bearing. In other words, eyes straight ahead, not to be looking all over the landscape, the proper length of arm-swinging, the proper length of stride and proper cadence to meet what at that time was the military pace of, I believe, 128 paces to the minute. So my military background was better suited to training young men totally unexposed to military life, than journalistic work, which certainly I could have done, but there were a lot of journalistic men available to the Navy.

Paul Stillwell: This was during the really big influx of recruits after the beginning of the war, so there was a great need to provide that training.

Mr. Dille: Oh, yes. They were building barracks for training camps like Great Lakes very strongly then because of this great influx.

Paul Stillwell: The marching and inspections and so forth strike me as a means of inculcating a sense of discipline and order-taking, rather than specific skills that would be needed on board ship.

Mr. Dille: Yes, that is correct. Perhaps most importantly, it instills a feeling of group oneness. The man marching beside me and in front of me and behind me is my brother, so to speak, and we are not individuals; we are formed into a unit that functions sometimes as a unit. Because of my military background, I was well qualified to command a military unit, for example, in a parade. From Great Lakes, several times I was the platoon commander for a parade drill platoon.

That was particularly fun when later I was involved with the black Navy personnel. *The Chicago Defender*, a daily black newspaper in Chicago, once a year puts on what they call Bud Billiken Day. It's a big celebration largely on the south side of

Chicago, down Michigan Avenue, but pretty close to the Loop, as well.* They have all kinds of activities in that. At least one year they wanted a drill platoon from Great Lakes Naval Training Station, and I commanded that platoon in the parade. I looked forward to it every bit as much as the men did. The weather was cool enough, so they were wearing dress blues but khaki leggings, and they had their round white hats squared away, as the Navy terms it—properly worn. Then it was a question of getting their rhythm and pace right during the marching itself. It was a very impressive drill unit, and it got lots of applause from the Chicago audiences.

Paul Stillwell: The point on unit cohesion is an important one, because I've heard a number of individuals say that when they got out into battle, they lost sight of being instruments of executing national policy and they were concerned instead about saving their buddies.

Mr. Dille: I think that after a certain amount of training, the cohesion does develop. I don't suppose it's on instinct; I suppose it's a reflex to given conditions of hazard, and the individual is apt to respond in a very prompt and effective and helpful way, which he probably would not if he not had that kind of background and training.

Paul Stillwell: How long did that assignment last before you got into public information?

Mr. Dille: I was in recruit training when the Navy announced that, for the first time in its history, it would accept general enlistments from Negroes.† Up until that time, they were limited to a few jobs within the Navy. A limited number were able to get into mechanic, machinery, machinist's mate line of work, but most were steward's mates or kitchen personnel, food preparation personnel.

Great Lakes Naval Training Station, like its companion stations, of which there were half a dozen scattered around the country, were suddenly to be inundated with large numbers of black recruits. This obviously brought up a great many elements of a new

---
* The Loop is the name of the business district in downtown Chicago.
† Black sailors first began moving into general service ratings in June 1942.

situation for the Navy administration, because it, I'm sure, came as something of a surprise to the command of the Navy. I'm sure that it was influenced strongly by President Roosevelt and his wife, Eleanor Roosevelt.[*] They were very sympathetic to and worked a good deal with the NAACP and the Urban League and those organizations that were pushing for greater and greater equality for the black person.[†]

Suddenly new barracks were being erected at Great Lakes. They made up a whole camp of, let's say, six or eight barracks buildings. I don't remember how many men that would house, but that's a lot of men. West of Green Bay Road, a whole new territory for Great Lakes Naval Training Station was established and named Camp Robert Smalls, because Robert Smalls was a black man who had been a hero in the Civil War.[‡] So the blacks were all assigned there. Of course, the segregation was obvious, and that raised a lot of questions. Nevertheless, that's the way the Navy ordered it, and that's the way the Navy did it.

I went to the recruit training commanding officer and said that I would like to be assigned to that camp.

Paul Stillwell: What motivated you to volunteer for that?

Mr. Dille: I suppose a combination of things, some selfish, some of a more generous feeling. If it was selfish motivation, it would be that perhaps it was an opportunity to distinguish myself in a new climate. It was a new territory where other officers might not do as well as I was sure I could, and therefore bring attention to myself, and therefore perhaps bring promotion.

Paul Stillwell: Why did you think you might do better than some others?

Mr. Dille: Because I would start with a friendly and sympathetic and understanding attitude toward them because of my past friendships with minority individuals. I also

---

[*] Franklin D. Roosevelt was President of the United States from 1933 to 1945.
[†] NAACP – National Association for the Advancement of Colored People.
[‡] Camp Robert Smalls was named for an escaped slave who captured the Confederate steamer *Planter* during the Civil War and turned her over to the U.S. Navy. He served as pilot of the *Planter* and later of the gunboat Keokuk.

genuinely felt that these men would need all of the help and understanding that could be mustered by the officers in charge of training them because of it being a whole new environment to them. There again, for them, an opportunity, if they would work at it.

Paul Stillwell: Had there been any blacks at all at Great Lakes before the establishment of Camp Robert Smalls?

Mr. Dille: Only in the capacities I mentioned earlier. There were a few petty officers, and there were a few chief petty officers, I believe, as chief machinist's mates. There were no black chief quartermasters, no black chief gunner's mates, no black coxswains or boatswains, what the Navy calls right-arm rating badges.* The others were all left-arm rating badges.

Paul Stillwell: Did they have a small area of their own?

Mr. Dille: No, they were mixed in wherever they were assigned. For example, if it was a black petty officer assigned to, let's say, a white recruit training division for some duty or other, he would be treated just as though he were white.

Paul Stillwell: He would be treated according to what his rating was.

Mr. Dille: Exactly. Whatever his responsibility was and what the duty assigned him was.

Paul Stillwell: It's curious that that pattern of integration didn't follow then with the large influx of blacks.

---

* Before and during World War II, a few enlisted men in the Navy's seagoing specialties were distinguished by wearing their rating badges on the right sleeves of their uniform jumpers. Included were such ratings as boatswain's mate, mineman, quartermaster, signalman, gunner's mate, turret captain, torpedoman's mate, and fire controlman.

Mr. Dille: Well, I think that numbers had a great deal to do with that. The Navy did not have a substantial percentage of black personnel at all throughout the whole Navy before this general enlistment came up. And for obvious reasons. Why would a black want to enlist in the Navy with so much foreclosed in the way of opportunity? Those who did understand it correctly and did approach it correctly and did enlist and get into machinist mate's schools and learn—for all practical purposes, call it learn a trade—found a niche for themselves and found progressive promotion for themselves. Those who went the steward's mates way and the kitchen way obviously were men without much ambition and men who felt that the main opportunities were foreclosed to them, and so they just went along as they were.

In terms of their billeting, I simply do not know whether or not there was any separate black housing prior to the declaration of war.

Paul Stillwell: The Navy had taken the step of integrating the general service ratings. Apparently it was considered too large a step to integrate the billeting as well, at the same time.

Mr. Dille: It would have required a lot of very artificial restructuring when you needed X number of brand-new buildings. The question then is, for the sake of integration, which was not favored by a great many people, you would otherwise have to take, say, many whites out of the barracks which they already occupied, move them over to the new ones, let's say, half those barracks, and then half blacks in those barracks. That, the Navy felt, would breed a whole lot of problems, a whole lot of troubles, and they didn't feel that was the way to approach it. Incidentally, it was my observation during my nearly four years in the Navy, that a surprising number of high-ranking naval officers, meaning, for the most part, Naval Academy graduates, were from the South. There were a lot of southerners. They had to take their orders from Congress, from the President, to accept these new general enlistments of blacks. But I'm sure that many, many of them did not want any part of it and therefore did not have a friendly, receptive attitude in trying to set up the necessary training to absorb them.

Paul Stillwell: You said you went to the commanding officer of the recruit training command. Who was that?

Mr. Dille: His rank was commander. He was a Naval Academy man, and he was simply responsible for all of the recruit training activities at Great Lakes, which was primarily a training station.

Paul Stillwell: I've heard the name Armstrong.[*]

Mr. Dille: Well, now, that's a little different. I'll conclude on the training. The recruit training commanding officer made all the assignments of officer personnel to the training activities. I went to him, as I said, and had asked to be assigned to the new black battalions.

Now, Daniel W. Armstrong was a Naval Academy graduate who did not stay in the Navy. He came from a distinguished family, basically a southern family, although I knew him very well, and I think he had a minimum of prejudice resulting from his geographical background. He also was a descendant of a man who founded—I'm quite sure I'm correct on this—Hampton Institute in Virginia, which was a college-level training for blacks.[†] So he was a natural choice for the Navy. There couldn't have been half a dozen like him in the entire country to call back to active duty and put in charge of this. So during all the years of the training of black recruits at the Great Lakes Naval Training Station, he was, with the rank of lieutenant commander, in charge of all that activity.[‡] He still reported to the commanding officer of the recruit training division of Great Lakes.

---

[*] Commander Daniel W. Armstrong, USNR, was officer in charge of Camp Robert Smalls. He was a 1915 Naval Academy graduate who resigned his regular commission after World War I and was recalled to active duty for World War II.

[†] Brigadier General Samuel Chapman Armstrong (1839-1893) served as a colonel of a black regiment in the Civil War, and that led to his interest in vocational education for black students. In 1868 he founded Hampton Normal and Agricultural Institute at Hampton, Virginia. His son Daniel was born in 1893, the year the father died.

[‡] Armstrong was promoted to commander while at Great Lakes and to captain after his departure for other wartime duty.

Paul Stillwell: Who was his boss, the commander?

Mr. Dille: I believe there were two involved. One's name was Edgar, and the one more active over a longer period was named Turek.* It was to Turek that I made my application. He had replaced Edgar by that time. Edgar had been ordered to some other assignment. Turek had advanced to command of the recruit training division.

Paul Stillwell: Did Armstrong have several subordinates of your rank?

Mr. Dille: Yes, yes. The basic structure of Camp Robert Smalls was four battalions of black recruits, each with a commanding officer, and they were with the rank of lieutenant (junior grade) or ensign. When I applied and asked for assignment over there, I was told that the Navy was assigning only Naval Academy graduates to that assignment, and they had a number of them available, because they had some sort of physical defect or problem, perhaps transitory, which prevented them from being ordered to sea. So they were used in that capacity. Commander Turek told me he was sorry. He could not put me over there, but he'd keep it in mind.

Well, one of the four men who had been put over there originally, suddenly—as a result, I guess, of exercises and training and medical care—eliminated his physical problem and was ordered to sea. Commander Turek called me and ordered me over there. I was an ensign. There was one lieutenant named Donald O. Van Ness, who was a Naval Academy graduate.† He had been out of the Navy but came back to active duty when the obvious framework of war was coming along. He was the number-one assistant to Commander Armstrong, and then there were four of us in command of the battalions. Each battalion broke down to companies. In my case, for example, I had a chief petty officer assigned to each company and several regular Navy petty officers, first class, second class, third, also assigned, and the requisite number of yeomen. I think we had three yeomen in the battalion office.

---

* Lieutenant Commander Harold B. Edgar, USN, was in charge of recruit training. Commander William Turek, USNR.
† Lieutenant Donald O. Van Ness, USNR, who had graduated from the Naval Academy in the class of 1935.

Paul Stillwell: Were these petty officers all white?

Mr. Dille: No, they were not. Most of them were white, simply because there weren't very many blacks who had made chief petty officers.

Paul Stillwell: When did you move into that assignment at Camp Robert Smalls?

Mr. Dille: I'd really have to look back into my books to be definitive on that. I'm going to guess March or so of '43.

Paul Stillwell: Were the black recruits given the same training that the white sailors on the main side were getting?

Mr. Dille: Oh, yes. Yes, they were.

Paul Stillwell: And part of that, I'm sure, would have been a testing program to determine aptitudes for various skills in the service.

Mr. Dille: Yes. Now, bear in mind this recruit training, under the pressures of war and the need for men, it was about an eight-week period of training. As you suggest, they were given tests for aptitudes and sent on then to appropriate schools for further training in the field in which they had aptitude. It was about that time in history when blacks could become signalmen or quartermasters or gunner's mates. And others chose the machinist branch, but if they had the aptitude and passed the test, they were sent on to those schools.

Paul Stillwell: I'm wondering if you could draw a comparison between the recruits. In that the blacks were coming in for the first time, I'm wondering if maybe the Navy was more selective with them, so they had a higher norm on these qualification tests than the whites at main side.*

Mr. Dille: I don't believe so. If so, I don't know of any study that was made of it, or that there was any way it was patently recognizable to the passer-by. I think that the quality of blacks who came into the Navy at that time was at least equal to the whites, because they'd been barred from it for so long. It looked like a new opportunity, something new.

Paul Stillwell: And I daresay they had a great deal of enthusiasm for it as a result.

Mr. Dille: Right. Right.

Paul Stillwell: And patriotism is a great motivator as well.

Mr. Dille: Yes.

Paul Stillwell: How much did you get together with your counterparts from the other battalions to discuss the way things were going?

Mr. Dille: Oh, very often. Commander Armstrong would hold meetings at least weekly to compare notes on problems, how they'd arisen, how they were best handled, and ideas for improving the training. So there were very regular meetings on that.

Paul Stillwell: Are there any specific problems or events that stand out in your mind?

Mr. Dille: No, certainly not with regard to training. No.

Paul Stillwell: Were the blacks given the same opportunities to go on liberty in the local community as whites were?

---

* As of February 1943, the Navy began receiving all its new recruits through conscription by the Selective Service. Prior to that the trainees had enlisted voluntarily.

Mr. Dille: Yes.

Paul Stillwell: Was there fence-building or cooperation sought with the local communities going along with this change?

Mr. Dille: This change in the racial acceptance?

Paul Stillwell: In bringing many more blacks on the station.

Mr. Dille: I'm taxing my memory a little bit. It seems to me that provisions were made for liberty, to let the men get into Chicago rather than flood the small local community. There was just a string of suburbs, starting at Great Lakes, being very small and progressively larger till you got down to Chicago. As I remember, it seemed best for everyone's sake to provide transportation. I believe that not only was there bus transportation, but I believe that the trains, the Northwestern Railroad ran immediately adjacent to Great Lakes, and also pulled into its main station on the west side of downtown Chicago. So that blacks, in their case, could get home to see family and visit for holiday if they had liberty.

Paul Stillwell: And if they weren't from that area, they could probably find their liberty recreation in the black community.

Mr. Dille: Yes, that's right. Which would not amount to much in the other communities between Chicago and Great Lakes.

Paul Stillwell: There were bound to be some disciplinary problems. I wonder if you could draw any comparison with your experience with the white recruits on the main side.

Mr. Dille: I hesitate to. I'm inclined to say that perhaps we had more disciplinary problems with the blacks, but only because they had been uprooted, so to speak, and cast into a totally new, strange and, in many respects, not particularly friendly environment than would be true of the whites. And among men who have quality or character or strength at all, this is apt to produce some rebellious activities. You'll get individuals who will be rebellious, and therefore require discipline. You were bound to have some who were simply against the system, who felt that the Navy wasn't really friendly to blacks now any more than it had been for its whole history up until then, so I think some of those things were inevitable. But I would not attribute them to a basic racial distinction.

Paul Stillwell: Many sailors of whatever race have an uncomfortable confrontation with reality when they find out what service life is like.

Mr. Dille: We had a few, but very limited number of instances where dope was involved, somebody bringing it on the station or a sailor getting in trouble ashore. This was not while he was there at Great Lakes, but getting in trouble in town, and having it turn out that he was under the influence. That happened a few times. And I suppose that the susceptibility of the blacks to that sort of thing was more than the whites, in general, although the same thing would happen occasionally with the whites too.

Paul Stillwell: Did you find yourself in the role of a counselor or father confessor for the men in your unit? Did they come to you individually at times?

Mr. Dille: A few. A few did voluntarily. A few others wound up cast in that sort of role after discipline had been imposed. With them it was more in the sense of pleading for leniency than asking me to be a father confessor or guide, though sometimes those roles will cross over.

Paul Stillwell: How did you select the leaders of the various subdivisions of the battalion?

Mr. Dille: I suppose, in a sense, they selected themselves. By that I mean that a limited number of individuals would distinguish themselves just in terms of their bearing and the way they looked, the way they acted, the way they respected military courtesy, the way they performed whatever duties they had, and, to the extent that they took tests, the way they performed on the tests.

Paul Stillwell: Do you remember any specific individuals from that period in terms of leadership quality?

Mr. Dille: One man who pops into my mind was named Duncan. He was a very good-looking man, a squad leader who had the bearing of a military man. His bearing, in terms of his ordering the squad to do this, that, or the other, was outstanding. He did not turn out to be one of the first officers; I don't know whether he ever became an officer, but he certainly went on to petty officer rank in a hurry and, I'm sure, performed very well to his own satisfaction and the Navy's.

Other than him, I'd be stretching to try to think of individuals.

Paul Stillwell: As time went on and you had the benefit of more experience, were you able to make improvements in administration of the black battalion?

Mr. Dille: I think only as a normal generic progress, just from the result of doing it more and more, over and over a period of time, if that's what you mean.

Paul Stillwell: I wonder if there might have been the application of any lessons learned in dealing with the black culture, for example, or specific things that might be accommodated to.

Mr. Dille: I think I'd be stretching to try to think. There may well have been. You'd think that there would be. Whether I'd do it individually or whether I'd try to think of it as my fellow officers would can be two different things. I'm sure in the case of officers with command of black recruits, starting with very little, if any, knowledge or friendships among minority groups—blacks, notably—many things would be surprises to them that would not be to me. But nothing of major philosophies or major restructuring that they could do. I think just in their own relationships, they would change a good deal.

Paul Stillwell: Did you have the assistance of chaplains in working with your battalion?

Mr. Dille: Mostly on Sunday, and there were regular services offered more often for those few who wanted more than just Sunday. Of course, that may be one aspect that is a little different. With a black unit, you are more apt to get a number who have come from the—oh, I don't know what the proper phrase would be—the singing, praising, shouting, and . . .

Paul Stillwell: More of an evangelistic fervor?

Mr. Dille: Yes, exactly. Exactly. Because I think there are more black churches who do favor that sort of recognition of services and activities, more expressive, really, more musical.

Paul Stillwell: Did you encourage sports and athletic participation in your battalion?

Mr. Dille: Sure. Yes, we had a lot of that. Most of the men participated. Of course, we were viewing that as physical training. However, we also had mandatory physical training, even to rope climbing.

Paul Stillwell: Was there a specific effort to use as instructors or company chief petty officers those who would be sympathetic to blacks or at least not have an overt prejudice against them?

Mr. Dille: I think certainly in terms of selection of chiefs and petty officers to perform with the black units, there was a very definite attempt to be sure that there was not an overt antipathy on the part of anyone.

Paul Stillwell: At what level was that selection made?

Mr. Dille: The personnel office of the Great Lakes Naval Training Station would make that selection. They might seek recommendations, if any were available, from Commander Armstrong or from any of us. Otherwise, they would just be by interviewing, or in giving the man the assignment, simply discussing with him what he was going to and what the assignment was, and either ask him, or try to sense whether or not there was any antipathetic reaction to the assignment. Otherwise, it was a matter of the assignment being made, and then if it was spotted later by one of us, having him reassigned.

Paul Stillwell: Were there many cases of that?

Mr. Dille: No, no. There were not. There were a few cases where such chiefs or petty officers had to be told that that attitude could not be displayed or that they must treat the men in the same fashion they would the whites or anywhere else they were. Otherwise, they would be reassigned, and usually that could be ironed out that way.

Paul Stillwell: It sounds as if the choice of Armstrong was a particularly good one. Can you recall any specific facets of his leadership?

Mr. Dille: I think it was a particularly good one, because he was a kind of a man of all seasons. He was a handsome man. Whether he was divorced or a widower, I'm not sure I remember, but he fitted into the Lake Forest high society framework very easily and very readily, which was a plus. See, the Ninth Naval District headquarters and other activities of the Ninth District were based at Great Lakes. Frequently the admiral was cultivating the local society, Lake Forest being the most conspicuously fashionable community of those on the North Shore. There were times when they would include Dan Armstrong with the admiral, and with some other high-ranking people, and I think it gave him an exposure, a kind of an inside track. And whether the admiral liked it or not, I think he would have to recognize that this man Armstrong was different, unusual, capable, a Naval Academy man, southern aristocracy, and should be listened to before spoken to.

Paul Stillwell: Were there any cases where that didn't happen, where he was spoken to without being given a chance to speak?

Mr. Dille: I can't think of any. Of course, naturally, his position was unique, and that would stir some resentment in terms of other officers of equal or even somewhat higher rank, at the attention he could get if he asked for it at the highest level.

I don't know what your schedule or agenda is, but I think you really want to get on to the officer situation, don't you?

Paul Stillwell: I certainly do.

Mr. Dille: It seems to me that that is a very interesting aspect.

The next major step, as far as my activities with the black minority constituents of the Navy, came when the Navy announced, to the great surprise of a great many people, that they were going to commission a dozen black officers. In that process, my understanding is that the Navy was pretty well screened. You had the entire United States Navy, wherever, here, aboard, wherever—screened for potential candidates.

For several reasons, this was very important to the Navy. The Navy recognized that the White House had a substantial interest in this kind of project. The Navy realized that it would look better if it did a good job of selecting the men, so that the men themselves could perform well and make the Navy look good. The result was that there were 16 men ordered to Great Lakes for training as officers.* These men arrived, and they were an extraordinary group. Here again, I quickly identified myself with the command at Great Lakes as someone interested in working with these men. I believed that I could be helpful primarily to indoctrinate these men in protocol, military courtesy, the new kind of relationship in which they would find themselves as commissioned

---

* Of the 16 black enlisted men who went through the training program, 13 eventually became officers. The other three remained enlisted men.

officers. In combining that information with my experience in recruit training and my military training, I felt that I could be helpful. I do not really remember the specifics of just how I got into the relationship with these men, or what my specific orders were, or what my specific capacity was. I think of it in terms of having been one of the very few officers responsible to a great degree for their training, to move from enlisted rank up to commissioned.

These were extraordinary men. Their degrees were from highly accredited universities; they were not, as some officers of the Navy might have feared or claimed, from small Negro colleges in the South. They were from institutions such as Howard University, which is primarily or solely a black university, an outstanding one in Washington, D.C. I know of degrees from the University of Chicago, which is my alma mater. In fact, one of these men was a classmate of mine at the University of Chicago and went on to take a law degree and then went on into the judicial system and is currently, although of retirement age, still on a significant bench in Chicago.[*]

Many of these men were athletes. A number of them would be perfectly at home on a platform, as master of ceremonies or speaking. They simply were superb. But they were going to face problems, and they knew it and I knew it. To the extent that I could be helpful, I tried to articulate these circumstances and set the warning signals up. It has been said in articles written about the Golden Thirteen that when they were first commissioned, there were enlisted men who would refuse to salute; others who would cross the street to avoid having to salute; others who simply thought they were impersonating officers. In fact, there's one instance that has been quoted of Samuel Gravely, when he was a younger officer, being arrested by the Navy's own shore patrol as an impersonator.[†]

Paul Stillwell: He told me about that.

---

[*] This was William Sylvester White, who at the time of this interview was a justice of the Illinois Appellate Court, one step below the state supreme court. Justice White retired from the bench in 1991.
[†] Vice Admiral Samuel L. Gravely Jr., USN (Ret.), was the Navy's first black flag officer. In one of the interviews for his Naval Institute oral history he told of being apprehended by military policemen when he was a junior officer. See Samuel L. Gravely Jr. with Paul Stillwell, *Trailblazer: the U.S. Navy's First Black Admiral* (Annapolis: Naval Institute Press, 2010).

Mr. Dille: Did he? Because these individuals didn't think the Navy had any such a thing as a black officer. Well, if anybody took a look at Sam Gravely later, a man of impressive physical dimensions, a man of very impressive bearing, later to become vice admiral and commander of the Third Fleet of the United States Navy, they'd be very quick and alert about saluting him, seeing him in his later years in the Navy.

So that was the beginning of my relationship to them in that capacity. They have been holding reunions for many years since and have been gracious enough to include me in their reunions. In fact, they have developed stationery. Have you seen that?

Paul Stillwell: Yes, I have a piece right here.

Mr. Dille: The design in the center is quite legible, although it doesn't spoil the stationery for typing. It says, "Thirteen plus one," and they've honored me by designating me the one.

Paul Stillwell: Justice White mentioned the names of two others who were in the training—Reginald Goodwin and Lewis Williams.[*] What do you remember of them?

Mr. Dille: Reginald Goodwin I knew particularly well, because he had been a yeoman with me for a substantial period of time.

Paul Stillwell: What was the story with Williams, who didn't make it?

Mr. Dille: I regret to say that while I remember Mummy Williams, and if I passed him on the street, I'd know him today, I do not remember the story on him. Was he not included in the picture or the list of names there?

---

[*] Reginald Ernest Goodwin was a member of the Golden Thirteen. He died before he could be interviewed by the Naval Institute's oral history program. Lewis Reginald Williams was one of the 16 black enlisted men selected to undergo officer training in early 1944. He was not commissioned and thus remained in enlisted status.

Paul Stillwell: No, and Justice White said that he felt bad, that Williams was the one who had gotten him into the Navy, and then he wasn't allowed to be commissioned at the same time that White was.

Mr. Dille: I remember Mummy Williams, but I can't answer the question as to why he wasn't commissioned. That would have to be answered by whatever individuals formed the group that selected them into the unit. I don't know what criteria they used. I only know the results they produced and the quality of the men that became commissioned being extraordinary.

Paul Stillwell: Goodwin, according to Justice White, was something of a liaison man. It was through him that the others transmitted their feelings to main side, and, in turn, he brought back the feelings of main side to that group.

Mr. Dille: That may very well be, although, again, I don't have a specific sense of that. Goodwin had been a yeoman, and I've forgotten to what petty officer rank he progressed when I last saw him, before he went to whatever duties he did and then became commissioned. But he was of a personality, of an affability, and of an appearance which probably created friendships of his own with a similar position of men—yeomen or chief yeomen—in the highest quarters. While I do not know specifically, that may be what the suggestion is, that that enabled him, through his own friendships, to learn things a little ahead of or earlier than we otherwise might have known.

Paul Stillwell: How was the curriculum developed for this group?[*]

Mr. Dille: Again, I think that would better be asked of one of them, because I was not involved in the curriculum. I'm not really even sure there was a curriculum per se.

Paul Stillwell: What did the training consist of, then?

---

[*] The curriculum was developed by Lieutenant (junior grade) Paul D. Richmond, USNR. See his chapter in Paul Stillwell, *The Golden Thirteen: Recollections of the First Black Naval Officers* (Annapolis: Naval Institute Press, 1993), pages 28-45.

Mr. Dille: Well, the part that I felt most involved in and interested in was indoctrination of conduct as a naval officer, anticipating the eligibility now, all of a sudden, for officers' clubs, the reaction of the current membership of officers' clubs, to suddenly having black officer members; the Navy regulations, in terms of how they applied to being an officer, how to conduct yourself among other officers, and, I suppose, general observations on when to speak and when to wait to be spoken to, and yet to accept gladly and proudly the full rank, as a commission indicates, and enjoy it. But I do not remember any formal curriculum.

Paul Stillwell: Did your indoctrination include special advice or training on the fact that they might not always be accorded the respect and courtesy that went with their new ranks?

Mr. Dille: Certainly, in discussion, yes. Formally, I never had anything written down to be sure to talk about this, because that would be inevitable to come up in discussion. More often than not, being the intelligent, educated, and, for the most part, sensitive men that they had to be to be qualified, they would anticipate those things and very well bring it up themselves, whether with me or among themselves. Or they might discuss it among themselves and then ask for reaction from me or from someone else involved in that training.

Paul Stillwell: Were you getting any policy guidance from your superiors on the treatment of the blacks, situations they might face as officers, or how they should be trained?

Mr. Dille: No. No. I may be thoroughly unfair, and I may be unjust, but from the beginning of their commissioned days, they had a feeling that higher ranking naval officers, particularly career officers—which means Naval Academy officers, for the most part—really felt that the less contact they could have with the whole subject, the better off they would be.

Again, I think some of the men themselves would give you much more perceptive and much more sensitive reactions to those situations, because they faced them; I did not.

Paul Stillwell: Did you counsel them to avoid confrontations if awkward situations did develop?

Mr. Dille: Oh, I don't think anything that I remember was discussed in that formal a sense. Like the other things, of what to anticipate, or what you might anticipate in officers' clubs or elsewhere, or officers' quarters, BOQs, here and around the world, I think, would be subjects that would just come up.[*] I remember more of just dialogues, just discussions, than I do of anything that would resemble a class or would resemble a formally structured thing.

Paul Stillwell: A great deal is made of marks in military training. What things were they graded on?

Mr. Dille: I don't remember any grading. By that time, of course, the only grading an officer gets is his fitness report.

Paul Stillwell: But during this training period to become officers, there would be grading.

Mr. Dille: I am just at a loss to remember or reconstruct that. Again, they would be far more competent to do it than I. I frankly don't really quite remember the specific conditions or how I arrived at the relationship in participating in their training.

Paul Stillwell: You said you had volunteered, as you had for the previous assignment. Was this an additional duty for you? Did you still have your battalion?

---

[*] BOQ – bachelor officers' quarters.

Mr. Dille: Oh, no. As I remember it, this was separate and of itself. Then it wasn't long after I became well acquainted with these men that I was ordered to the Pacific, because the Navy wanted more recognition of what the blacks were doing, and that meant public relations. So I was ordered to the ComServPac, Commander Service Force Pacific Fleet, where the senior public relations officer told me, in effect, "You can have just about anything you want, but get some pictures and stories back to the American press that show and say that these sailors are doing well in the Navy and are performing worthwhile missions."

It was a long war. See, in between these two activities, I was ordered from Great Lakes to the Hawaiian Islands in command of Ordnance Battalion Number One, which was largely black. There were three white officers assigned with me. I was at that time a lieutenant. One lieutenant (junior grade) and two ensigns were assigned as part of my organization, ordered to what was called Waikele Gulch, NAD Oahu, naval ammunition depot. It was up in the mountains north of Honolulu and really up above a little town called Waipahu. The Navy had blasted tunnels into the sides of the mountains in the valley going up, and in those tunnels were stored torpedoes. I think I am correct in saying—it certainly was true up until the time I got there and until I left—that we handled all the torpedoes for the Pacific Fleet. That was a different function; then came the public relations.

Paul Stillwell: Did you stay at Great Lakes until the 13 men were commissioned?

Mr. Dille: No, I was gone by the time they were commissioned.

Paul Stillwell: Were you disappointed that you couldn't be around for that?

Mr. Dille: Oh, well, yes. But, of course, things moved so fast in your own activities and your own life, that there were a lot of disappointments in one way or another.

Paul Stillwell: Did you pass on that responsibility to another individual?

Mr. Dille: No, I was not that directly responsible for it. Really, they can tell you much better than I how it began, what, if any, structured curriculum there was, what grading, as you asked, there was, and what or who made the determination that they were qualified to be commissioned.

Paul Stillwell: Justice White had the perception that before commissioning, they were shunted off in a corner, so if they failed, they would fail in secret. Is that your memory of it?

Mr. Dille: No. I think that's more psychological than physiological. That may be his feeling.

Paul Stillwell: He thought they weren't given much publicity, so that if they didn't do well, the Navy wouldn't be embarrassed.

Mr. Dille: Well, that may very well be, but that is nothing that I would think they should be sensitive to, because other than having been named and announced that they were going to, as a journalist, I don't know that they would be worthy of much publicity until it was completed. I think that may be hypersensitive on his part.

Paul Stillwell: I'd like to run through the names of the 13 and get your individual memories of each one.

Mr. Dille: Oh, my. You're really asking for something.

Paul Stillwell: Well, if you don't, we'll just pass.

Mr. Dille: First give me something a little more definitive. What do you mean by my memories of them?

Paul Stillwell: Well, you talked about personalities. You talked about Goodwin in terms of having the yeoman connection. Justice White mentioned Dennis Nelson as a very proud man.[*]

Mr. Dille: Dennis Nelson was a very proud man. Of course, I liked every one of them. Dennis Nelson I liked, but he would be one of the ones I would find most easy to get into an argument with. And that's to his credit, because he was always a positive person. He knew what he felt, and he articulated it. And he did it very, very well. I remember so clearly when I raised the question one time about, "Geez, all of a sudden, you guys are calling yourselves black and everyone else is calling you black. I would have been thrown out of my own home by my mother if I'd used that term, when 'Negro' or 'colored' was the accepted term."

Dennis said, "Jack, I'll say it to you, but I'll say it to anyone else, too. I am not black, and I don't want to ever be called black." He felt very strongly on that subject. Some of the others, I think, just shrugged their shoulders and would just take it as a meaningless identification that the world, as it exists, suddenly had taken upon itself to use.

Paul Stillwell: I take it this is a thing he said in later years.

Mr. Dille: Yes, in later years.

Paul Stillwell: What do you remember of Jesse Arbor?[†]

Mr. Dille: Jesse Arbor is a very gregarious individual. He was then and he still is. He's fun to be with.

Paul Stillwell: Very loquacious.

---

[*] Dennis Denmark Nelson II eventually retired from the Navy as a lieutenant commander. He died in 1979 before he could be interviewed as part of the Naval Institute's oral history program.
[†] Ensign Jesse Walter Arbor, USNR, was a member of the Golden Thirteen. His oral history is in the Naval Institute collection.

Mr. Dille: Yes, indeed. And if you want to really get a subject exhausted or even well and thoroughly treated, you'd better stay right with it before Jesse brings some other subject into play. But anything he does, he'll do it with a laugh and always with great kindness.

Paul Stillwell: Phillip Barnes.

Mr. Dille: Phillip Barnes I probably knew much less well than the others.[*] There are a few that I really never spent enough time with on a one-to-one basis to form much of an opinion. He has not been one who has been active in the reunions since.[†] My memory of him at that time, I had no particular impression.

Paul Stillwell: Samuel Barnes.

Mr. Dille: Samuel Barnes was and is a very active, very progressive leadership type of individual.[‡] He showed that in the Navy and he has shown it in private life. He's a good organizer, and he will participate in any activity that he thinks is good and wholesome and proper, and he'll do a good job of it.

Paul Stillwell: Dalton Baugh.

Mr. Dille: Dalton Baugh—I don't know how much engineering he had had.[§] I suppose he had college; I suppose his degree was in engineering. He may have had more than one degree. Engineering was certainly his later life background. He was obviously leadership quality. He was able and willing to express himself at any time or on any occasion where he felt it appropriate, and yet had the grace and judgment not to press it unless it would serve a beneficial purpose.

---

[*] Phillip George Barnes was a member of the Golden Thirteen.
[†] Phillip Barnes died in the 1950s, prior to the time when the members of the Golden Thirteen began holding reunions.
[‡] Samuel Edward Barnes was a member of the Golden Thirteen. His oral history is in the Naval Institute collection.
[§] Dalton Louis Baugh was a member of the Golden Thirteen. He died in 1985, before he could be interviewed by the Naval Institute's oral history program.

Paul Stillwell: George Cooper.

Mr. Dille: George Cooper is certainly one of the outstanding men of the group.* His general demeanor, the grace with which he moves and conducts himself—I don't mean that entirely in a physical sense, but the role he plays as a man among men is, to me, very impressive, and I think he was destined to be a leader from childhood.

Paul Stillwell: What do you mean about the man among men? Is he a take-charge type of an individual?

Mr. Dille: I'm not comfortable with that phrase, because that phrase "take charge" sounds like presumption or seizing upon an opportunity to take charge, and I don't mean that at all. I simply mean that I think anyone of balance would recognize in him the leadership quality and the kind of appearance which would attract you to him if you felt that you needed something done by him or needed his opinion on something.

Paul Stillwell: Reginald Goodwin.

Mr. Dille: Reginald Goodwin, of course, is gone now.† And I was very sorry to lose contact with him. We kept contact after the war for a while. Before the commissioning, probably I knew him better than any of the others, and on a number of occasions, since my home was so close by, he came to my home in Highland Park and visited with me and my wife. He could have been a great politician, but I mean that in the nicest sense of the term. He had a natural affinity for people and related to people and sensed their relationship to him about as well as anybody I have known.

Paul Stillwell: James Hair.

---

* George Clinton Cooper is a member of the Golden Thirteen. His oral history is in the Naval Institute collection.
† Goodwin died in 1974.

Mr. Dille: Jim Hair was perhaps physically the most attractive of the group—depending on what standards you use for good looks.* During those years, at least, he was quiet, but then and to this day he is very warm and expressive about friendships.

Paul Stillwell: Charles Lear.

Mr. Dille: Charles Lear I really didn't know well enough.† He was physically a fine specimen, and he certainly had leadership qualities. I gathered from his being brought in with the group without a college degree that he must have had leadership qualities that the Navy itself recognized in whatever assignments he had prior to that time. Beyond that, I was not close enough to him.

Paul Stillwell: Graham Martin.

Mr. Dille: Graham Martin is extraordinary in the sense of a man whose background, only one generation back, went to towns like Tobacco Port, Tennessee.‡ He came from the most rural and the most unrefined of backgrounds in terms of heredity and history, and yet he was an outstanding athlete. He played football as a tackle for Indiana University, an outstanding one, and he wasn't there just on an athletic scholarship. He also made good grades, because he's the kind of a man who knew that that would be important to him later. He also played on the Great Lakes Naval Training Station football team. If you know anything about the World War II days of that football team, it was about as All-American, about as top as you could get. They had some of the greatest stars of history on it, and he played on that team.

Graham is very quiet, devoted to his family. His wife is crippled, yet she comes to our reunions. She's really in a wheelchair mostly now, but he's as attentive to her as

---

* James Edward Hair was a member of the Golden Thirteen; his oral history is in the Naval Institute collection. In 1945 he became the first black officer in the destroyer escort *Mason* (DE-529), a ship with an all-black enlisted crew. Hair died in 1992.
† Charles Byrd Lear was a member of the Golden Thirteen. He died shortly after World War II.
‡ Graham Edward Martin was a member of the Golden Thirteen. His oral history is in the Naval Institute collection.

can be. He does not speak much unless you let him know that you're interested in his opinion, and if you do, he'll give it, and it will be very logical; it will seem very, very sound. Probably the most unusual, in the sense of what he started with and what he wound up with in the whole group.

Paul Stillwell: Did you have any other recollections of Dennis Nelson from back in his time in officer training?

Mr. Dille: Other than what I've already said, only that he was kind of a human spark plug. He was a man who activated things. Sometimes they led to dissension; sometimes they led to constructive criticism, but almost always they were just as well brought up and disposed of.

Paul Stillwell: John Reagan.

Mr. Dille: John Reagan is another I did not know as well as I knew some of them.[*] I would call him a rather quiet member of the group. Again, he was of physical stature that was impressive. In fact, he played Canadian football at one time. I think that's really about all I remember about John.

Paul Stillwell: Frank Sublett.

Mr. Dille: Frank Sublett.[†] I think I just had a letter from him. It just came in a couple of days ago. A very engaging personality, very good-looking man, very articulate. I think he was one who was always willing and ready to participate in dialogue of any kind.

Paul Stillwell: William White.

---

[*] Ensign John Walter Reagan, USNR, was a member of the Golden Thirteen. His oral history is in the Naval Institute collection.
[†] Frank Ellis Sublett Jr. was a member of the Golden Thirteen. His oral history is in the Naval Institute collection.

Mr. Dille: William Sylvester White. Well, perhaps he's the most prestigious in terms of his academic background and his years since. As I indicated earlier, he was a classmate of mine at the University of Chicago, the class of '35, although we did not know each other at that time. It's a big university. Both of us later did graduate work. I stopped after a master's degree; he went on and finished his law degree and has been in that field ever since. He is very analytical, certainly wanted always to keep things moving in his own career, but also in the Golden Thirteen, and sometimes expressed himself as feeling that the Golden Thirteen ought to have something more purposeful to be doing than just having reunions, for example. But I think this was simply meant as a constructive suggestion more than criticism, but typical of a searching mind. I think that's what brought him to his naval commission, and that's what has brought him to the eminence of his mature career.

Paul Stillwell: You perhaps, as an outsider, might be in the best position to comment on the relationship among these individuals. They're all top-notch people. Were they competitive with each other as a group?

Mr. Dille: I think there really were no circumstances that I'm familiar with that would give evidence of that kind of competitiveness. I think that in the way I have known them and while they were candidates for commissions and so on, I would call them much more supportive of one another than competitive. They had many things in common, including their leadership capacity, but also whatever problems or handicaps go with being born to a minority, as they were. I would say more supportive than anything. Now, cast in roles where they might be striving for, say, the same command or the same position, it might be a different story. But they'd approach it differently, quite differently, because their personalities are quite different. There would be the few who would exhibit the tiger approach to being competitive, and others who would use the study, study, research, come to a conclusion, then push it type.

Paul Stillwell: Are there any you want to identify as the potential tigers?

Mr. Dille: No, I don't think that would be quite fair. There are several who have the capacity. Whether they would exercise it or not is something else.

Paul Stillwell: Do you know how the name Golden Thirteen originated?

Mr. Dille: No, I really do not. No, I do not know.

Paul Stillwell: Is there anything else to say about them before we resume the description of your career in the Pacific?

Mr. Dille: I think I've covered them pretty well, but I'll always be looking forward to their reunions and hoping as many of us can survive to continue them as possible.

Paul Stillwell: You said you went out specifically to bring to public notice the accomplishments of black Navy men.

Mr. Dille: Right. And the Navy, at my request, searched for some men who were experienced as black journalists, who had worked either for black newspapers or white. About the middle of 1944 or the latter part of 1944, I had put together several such men and a couple of photographers. Then I had the cooperation of the Commander Service Force and was able to locate where blacks were performing in different kinds of Navy activities, where we could get a story and/or pictures on them. So we began that in the Hawaiian Islands and then covered a lot more territory in the process. CinCPac, Commander in Chief Pacific, was at Guam, and so I moved on out to Guam. We covered activities in Guam, Tinian, Saipan--the Marianas group--and we went to the Philippines, Samar and Leyte, and covered activities of black Navy men there. We produced many pictures and stories about the men and what they were doing.

Paul Stillwell: Were those released from CinCPac headquarters?

Mr. Dille: Yes.

Paul Stillwell: Did you go through Fitzhugh Lee as the press officer?

Mr. Dille: Yes. Yes, Fitzhugh Lee—incidentally, another aristocratic southern Naval Academy man, a very fine officer.[*]

Paul Stillwell: Was he supportive of your efforts?

Mr. Dille: Yes, he was very supportive. And Roger White was another one, not as high rank as Fitz Lee.[†] Yes, I had nothing but cooperation.

As a matter of fact, other problems that arose are interesting, not bearing on what I was doing specifically, but where I was able to be of help. Enoch Waters was a very fine newspaperman whom I knew because he was a Chicagoan and he was with *The Chicago Defender*. And a man named Charlie Loeb was a war correspondent for the *Courier* and a group of black newspapers. They came to Guam to perform their chores for their own newspapers, and they were housed in barracks with some black personnel. Obviously, they were both black. In talking to me, they said, "Well, we can't work normally, Jack. Normally we would be in the BOQ, where the other correspondents are, and that's where we all get together and compare notes and get ideas and give ideas and so on. But here we're stuck off to the side."

I said, "Let me see if I can do anything about that." So I went to whoever my superior was in that capacity regarding press, and explained this. He sent a memorandum at my request to the vice admiral who was Admiral Nimitz's chief of staff. I believe his name was McMorris, known as Soc McMorris, and he was a Naval Academy southern man.[‡] He sent back the memorandum regarding Enoch Waters and Charlie Loeb and said, "This is addressed to the admiral," meaning the commander in chief, and he said, "I will not bother the admiral with such trivia."

That came back to me. So I did another memorandum and got it back up to McMorris's staff, chief aide, and said, "With great regret, the admiral expresses this as

---

[*] In April 1945 Captain Fitzhugh Lee, USN, became public relations officer on the staff of Fleet Admiral Chester W. Nimitz, USN. The oral history of Lee, who retired as a vice admiral, is in the Naval Institute collection.
[†] Lieutenant Commander Roger Q. White, USNR.
[‡] Vice Admiral Charles H. McMorris, USN, was from Alabama.

trivia, but I can assure you from knowledge that you would have no reason to possess, but I do, that this would not be considered trivia in the White House with *the* commander in chief."* And that made an impression. So Charlie and Enoch wound up in the BOQ. That was one of those side issues, but they're problems that the minority individuals must overcome to achieve. In many ways, I would say they have to be superior to their white counterparts to achieve any reasonable parity.

Paul Stillwell: Did you have two types of material, one targeted toward a general audience and one specifically to the black media?

Mr. Dille: No, no, I didn't think, and apparently the viewpoint was supported, it should be done just as the media would do it. That is, as general reporters would prepare releases for the media, hoping that quality would be recognized by the white media and having no doubt but that the black media would pick it up.

Paul Stillwell: Did you have a means of assessing your effectiveness in getting the stories printed?

Mr. Dille: Yes, limited to the requests made constantly that the Washington big public relations office, which has clipping services, keep an eye out and clip, as best they could, whatever they found on this subject. I have a bunch of clippings there now. White papers picked up some—nothing like the black. Black papers picked them all up. We were more successful there, but that was of value to the Navy, too, which was our purpose, and those white papers that did, it was very helpful to have.

Paul Stillwell: Any other recollections from that time you were in the Pacific?

Mr. Dille: No, I would have to say, despite the weaknesses in its operations that I have expressed with this particular subject, I was impressed constantly at the quality at the Navy's command and structure and execution. In 1945, after V-J Day, I was able to

---

* This is a reference to President Roosevelt.

make contact with the Washington headquarters and request assignment to return to assemble some of the journalism work that had been done, and got it.* So I was fortunate to get orders back to the United States quite soon after the war itself had ended. So I got back to my family in much better and shorter time than most men were able to.

Paul Stillwell: Were the black men that you reported on substantially in segregated units?

Mr. Dille: No, we tried, as far as possible, to get them aboard ship as well as shore-based, but aboard ship as much as possible. Now, we were not able to get as many on combat ships as we were on service force ships, but they were performing valuable and definite capacities, of which they could be proud and which could be respected for their contributions to the war effort.

Paul Stillwell: What was your rank at the end of the war?

Mr. Dille: I was a lieutenant, which is equivalent to captain in the Army, at the time the war ended. Then I was promoted in the reserve very shortly thereafter. My fitness reports had come in, and they were good. I was promoted to lieutenant commander, and shortly thereafter, I got out of the reserve. That was the end of that.

Paul Stillwell: Any overall summations of your naval experience to conclude this?

Mr. Dille: No. I think I've covered about as many as are reasonable. I'm just glad we won the war.

Paul Stillwell: Thank you very much for your time and sharing your recollections, because you were indeed involved in a historic project and, in part through your efforts, it succeeded.

---

* V-J Day - Victory over Japan Day, marking the end of the war in the Pacific on 15 August 1945.

Mr. Dille: Well, I'm flattered that you and your institute were interested enough in wanting my points of view.

Paul Stillwell: Thank you.

Interview Number 2 with Mr. John F. Dille Jr.

Place: Mr. Dille's office at Federated Media, Elkhart, Indiana

Date: Friday, 25 August 1989

Interviewer: Paul Stillwell

Paul Stillwell: It's a pleasure to see you again, Mr. Dille. Since our last meeting, I've had a chance to interview all of the surviving Golden Thirteen members, which was not the case the first time. So I have some more background, and I think there are some areas to fill in from our first interview. Before we started today, you gave me some additional information about your certification for getting an officer's commission. I think that would be interesting for the record.

Mr. Dille: Well, it's a pleasure to see you again. I think it's a commendable project you're engaged in here. Certainly the Golden Thirteen and survivors thereof are worth the attention you're giving them.

At the time of Pearl Harbor, December 7, 1941, I was living with my family in Highland Park, Illinois, and felt that with the Pearl Harbor attack that I was inclined to serve, and my choice of services was the Navy. The Navy required a college degree at that time to be commissioned as an officer, and while I had had four years at the University of Chicago, I was just a little bit short of the full and final qualifications for a bachelor's degree, which I completed later, and then went on to a master's degree from there.

But at the time this was something of a problem since I wanted the Navy rather than any other branch of service. I wrote to the president of the University of Chicago, Robert Maynard Hutchins, and explained my situation to him. I reminded him of some of the activities I had participated in at the university and asked him for a recommendation that the Navy waive the formal requirement of a college degree. I wanted the Navy to accept his recommendation that I had, at least, equal of that and perhaps more in terms of what would be required of a naval officer.

He was gracious enough to honor my request, and part of the language he used was, "With the interests of the Navy in mind, I am able to give this recommendation, not only because Mr. Dille was an active member of our student body between 1931 and '35, but because I have had sufficient personal contact with him in recent years to know of leadership qualities which he has displayed in military training instruction here at the university, in alumni affairs, in his business, and in preparedness activities in the interest of national defense."

The Navy was very happy to accept that recommendation, and so I was commissioned.

Paul Stillwell: What was the date of his letter?

Mr. Dille: The date of President Hutchins's letter was January 22, 1942. During the next 60 days or so, the Navy Department in Washington apparently considered President Hutchins's letter and acknowledged the request for the waiver. I was commissioned shortly thereafter and ordered to active duty at Great Lakes Naval Training Station on April 13, 1942.

Paul Stillwell: I know it's not directly related to the Golden Thirteen, but I'd be interested in hearing more on the role of the battalion commander in the boot camp setup. We discussed that briefly before.

I remember when I was in boot camp, the key man for the recruits was the active duty chief petty officer, who ran the company. I'm wondering what the relationship was between you and the company commanders.

Mr. Dille: Well, the organizational structure, certainly in the case of the newly enlisted black recruits at Camp Robert Smalls, was four battalions, as I remember it. Each battalion had several companies, let's say four, and the battalion commander was a commissioned officer. And you're correct, the company commander was a chief petty officer. In the case of the setup for the black enlisted men, the four battalion commanders reported to Lieutenant Commander Daniel Armstrong, who was on special assignment for that purpose.

Paul Stillwell: You did not have, I would guess, that much direct contact with the recruits. What was your specific role in this structure?

Mr. Dille: Well, it primarily was to see that the company commanders, the chief petty officers, carried out the formula for training. It was a well-specified formula on different kinds of training—some physical, some in terms of learning Navy language, and Navy procedures. We had to be sure that the classes were held, and that the physical activities were carried out thoroughly and efficiently.

Paul Stillwell: How did you monitor that progress?

Mr. Dille: Well, by being present, by actually visiting the various companies, listening to and watching the chief petty officers at work and the subordinate petty officers under them, who worked throughout the companies—some in terms of special training, some in terms of disciplinary training.

Paul Stillwell: Did you have some means for dealing with those recruits who weren't performing satisfactorily?

Mr. Dille: Well, I don't know that it could be considered a systematic procedure of any kind. You will always have in military units a small percentage of men—and in these days, I guess women, too—who cannot or will not—more often will not perform up to standards set by the Navy. Disciplinary procedures in the cases of those who just were arbitrarily not making the effort would be to cancel the number of periods of liberty they have to go ashore for entertainment or visiting, to get off the station and back in at night. Or more severe disciplinary efforts could be made in terms of just raw physical work required.

Paul Stillwell: For those who didn't have the aptitude, there must have been procedures also.

Mr. Dille: Well, I think our remedy would be not be formally recognized by educational institutions, but there were additional classes held for these men to try to stimulate their interests, or point out to them that if they would make the effort, that this was not that difficult to accomplish. In most cases it worked pretty well.

Paul Stillwell: One problem that I've heard mentioned from members of the Golden Thirteen was illiteracy among some of the black recruits. They told me that a remedial reading program was established. Did you observe that?

Mr. Dille: I don't remember having any intimate contact with it at all. That's a pretty difficult procedure to carry out in a period of weeks, when the recruit is at a training command. And while the periods varied, I think, from, say, 8 to 12 weeks, after that length of time, unless held back, the sailor would be assigned to a regular Navy unit somewhere and would be out of your control. So it could not be a very effective remedial reading program, although efforts were made.

Paul Stillwell: To what extent did you observe patriotism as a motivator for the recruits at Camp Robert Smalls?

Mr. Dille: Well, I had not thought of that particular factor.

Paul Stillwell: Well, it was sort of curious that here was a country that denied the black men many opportunities, and yet had the same expectations for them as for whites once they got in the military service.

Mr. Dille: Well, yes, but I think my feeling is that the blacks' reaction to discrimination would be aimed at the racial discriminators, specifically, mostly the whites, rather than anything to do with the Navy.

I think their feeling for the beauty of the flag, and the spirit of the flag, and the teamwork called for by the flag was very high. It was as much as it would be, say, in athletics and sports. It was a team effort, and it was, I think, just as important to them as to anyone else—if the subject was given thought at all—that our country prevail over the enemy. And, of course, all blacks as well as the whites considered the Pearl Harbor bombing as a dastardly act. They were just as anxious as anyone else, not necessarily to get even, but certainly to assure this country's security by prevailing over the Japanese.

Paul Stillwell: Certainly a milestone event was in June of 1942, when the general service ratings were opened to the blacks. It's interesting that an external threat of war is what opened up the internal opportunity for the black sailors.

Mr. Dille: Yes, well, that's one way to phrase it, Paul; however, there were lots of other motivations, which I would not attach to patriotism or the threat of an enemy as much as to the insistence of important elements within this country who were demanding equality and the reasonable fairness of treatment. I think that that had a great deal to do with the opening up of general enlistments. Plus the fact that to those who gave it proper thought, the black population offered a lot of valuable manpower, which was not being utilized properly until they were given an opportunity to do something other than the menial jobs—in the Navy, particularly. The Navy was the notable service for holding them back in that sense.

Paul Stillwell: Could you perhaps articulate the attitude that your fellow white officers held towards blacks in the Navy in 1942?

Mr. Dille: Well, it's hard to speak for others.

Paul Stillwell: I'm wondering what you observed, though, in your conversations with your colleagues.

Mr. Dille: Well, I suppose as a generalization, the white commissioned officers did not welcome the opening of general enlistments to the blacks or the potential advancement of blacks to petty officer grades and later as commissioned officers. Certainly that was not uniform. In any society in which you participate, you'll get different opinions. And certainly mine did not fall into that category.

I believe I'm correct in saying that a surprising percentage of Naval Academy graduates are southerners. And Naval Academy graduates, in general, dominate the service. When you get up to the Chief of Naval Operations and the fleet commanders, the top administrative positions, as well as combatant positions, I believe you'll find they are largely, if not entirely, Naval Academy graduates. Today there are exceptions, notably the black vice admiral, Sam Gravely, who has participated in our reunions with the Golden Thirteen. He was a V-12 product.[*]

Paul Stillwell: Yes, he was.

Mr. Dille: But that was World War II; that was the exception and rare. Largely Naval Academy graduates held the high positions, and I'm quite sure I'm correct that a surprising percentage of them were southerners. Jimmy Carter, for example, is one name that comes to mind.[†]

Paul Stillwell: There was, of course, a geographical distribution in that congressmen all over the country made nominations for appointments for Naval Academy midshipmen.

Getting onto the Golden Thirteen, specifically, what do you remember about the physical setup of their barracks, classroom, and so forth?

Mr. Dille: I really hesitate to try to reconstruct my memory on that. I would rather leave that to the Golden Thirteen themselves since you have access to their opinions. Since

---

[*] During World War II, V-12 was a Naval Reserve officer training program in which individuals received naval instruction at the same time they worked toward bachelor's degrees. The program, which was held at civilian colleges and universities, took about two years. See James G. Schneider, *The Navy V-12 Program: Leadership for a Lifetime* (Boston: Houghton Mifflin, 1987).
[†] James E. Carter of Georgia graduated from the Naval Academy in the class of 1947 and later served as President of the United States from 1977 to 1981.

they were the actual participants in it, they would be far more accurate and more complete than I could be.

Paul Stillwell: Did you have occasion to visit their barracks, or did they come to you?

Mr. Dille: I do not remember actually visiting their quarters. For the most part, my contact with them would be in the process of training them to become officers, whether it would be in a drill or classroom.

Paul Stillwell: I gathered that their classroom was in their barracks, so did that mean that you went to that classroom?

Mr. Dille: I guess it must have. You're going back a lot of years for me, and I'm not really that clear. I'd rather they would answer that.

Paul Stillwell: They all remember you very warmly, and as being an exception to most of those whom they encountered among the white officers. Do you have an explanation for that?

Mr. Dille: My reaction is to believe that, number one, I grew up in a family, which was about as free of prejudice, I think, as an American family can be. My mother was a very active member of the Daughters of the American Revolution and was a chapter president of that in Chicago. She was as willing to love any human being, black skin as she would be the red skin, or a white skin, largely depending on how that individual reacted to her or conducted himself or herself. Secondly, I grew up most of my grade school years and all my high school years in Evanston, Illinois, which had a very substantial, and for the most part, a very wholesome black community. It had its own pride and a matter of self-discipline and cooperation with the city government and other elements of the society and community. I went to Evanston High School, which was a very large high school, and I had a lot of black classmates. Friendships developed there with blacks, just as well as among the whites. It may have been a little bit different background from a lot of white officers.

Paul Stillwell: Did you have the sense that black officer candidates could confide in you, whereas, they could not in other white officers?

Mr. Dille: I would hesitate to go that far because in the handful of officers we had involved with the black units, there were some men of sterling character and, possibly, somewhat more prejudiced, or let's say, less free of prejudice than I. But in terms of confidentiality, I don't remember one of them assigned to that duty who couldn't have been confided in by one of the men.

Paul Stillwell: Well, the sense I got talking to the men of the Golden Thirteen is that they trusted you, and they felt that you were legitimately concerned in helping them to succeed.

Mr. Dille: Well, if there is credit to be given, I would certainly give it to my mother or the way I grew up, perhaps a feeling of sensibility for the problem of the other person. I think perhaps I felt much more keenly than most others the problems that would arise for these men in assuming a brand-new role in history. It required assimilation by an element that simply was not used to having new sorts of things.

Paul Stillwell: A key man in this was Commander Armstrong, and we did discuss him previously. I wonder if you have any more that you can recall about his role in that regard because he was so important.

Mr. Dille: No, I had a high regard for Dan Armstrong. You have recorded his history and his orientation to blacks in terms of what his family had done in the educational institutions. Obviously, he would have a sympathetic background. He was a Naval Academy graduate who was very much a southern gentleman. I think he conducted himself very, very well under various kinds of extraordinary pressure.

Paul Stillwell: The southern gentleman background apparently led at least some of the Golden Thirteen to perceive him as condescending toward them. Were you aware of that attitude they had toward him?

Mr. Dille: I can understand how they would have that attitude. I would not recognize it as such, but I can certainly feel for their reactions. After all, here's a man who was reared in a multi-generation family in the South. The family obviously went back to slave days and would view the role of the blacks as not quite the same as the role of the whites in society.

Paul Stillwell: At least somewhat patronizing, perhaps.

Mr. Dille: Yes, I suppose it would appear to be patronizing and somewhat condescending. I think it might have been difficult, if not impossible, for him not to have been in some ways, although he certainly made every effort to be fair. And he fought hard for the equipment and for the facilities, the opportunity to progress in the Navy for the blacks.

Paul Stillwell: I would really welcome any specific examples you recall along those lines of things that he did fight for that were useful.

Mr. Dille: Well, I think I'd be getting myself into territory that is difficult to be sure of my memory on. Not that I would not be willing to try, but I really would be partly speculating. There were so many, so many matters that came along. I think I'd have a difficult time specifying. Some of the others, some of the Golden Thirteen, may remember.

Paul Stillwell: Do you have any examples of his fairness?

Mr. Dille: Only as a generalization. I thought he was a very fair man. He had four of us as commissioned officers reporting to them. Certainly I never had any feeling that he was being anything but fair and helpful, and aware of the needs of the black personnel.

Paul Stillwell: Was it in your view a completely good-faith effort on Commander Armstrong's part to have a successful program for the black officer candidates?

Mr. Dille: There again, I don't remember the respective roles that we played in working with these specially selected men to become commissioned officers. I wish that some of the Golden Thirteen would enlighten us on just what the roles were. Of the four officers—five, including Commander Armstrong—I don't remember the specific roles we played as far as these officer candidates were concerned. In fact, I would like to have George Cooper, or one of the others, tell me why he remembers that my role was different from Commander Armstrong's, Lieutenant Van Ness's, Lieutenant (junior grade) Richmond's.*

Paul Stillwell: I don't think they see it as a difference in role but a difference in attitude.

Mr. Dille: Were we all involved in the training? That's what I'm not clear in my own mind, on the training and manpower.

Paul Stillwell: That I don't know. I'm sure there was a difference in attitude. I have talked with Captain Van Ness. I think he was carrying out his orders because that was the code of a naval officer. But it was not something that he really wanted to do, and he said it was not something that he would want to do again.

Mr. Dille: Well, of course, there again, you have a Naval Academy graduate. I assume that when you go to the Naval Academy, you have in mind becoming a professional naval officer. That means that the finest thing you can do is go to sea and command a

---

* Lieutenant (junior grade) Paul D. Richmond, USNR, was the officer who devised the specific training curriculum for the black officer candidates. His oral history on the subject is in the Naval Institute collection.

ship. I would suspect that in the back of the mind of any such man from the Naval Academy, and that, of course, includes Armstrong, Van Ness, and Richmond—they all went to the Naval Academy—that there might be that feeling that they were sidetracked as far as what they really would have liked to have done.

Paul Stillwell: Did you have any contact with the instructors or the curriculum that the Golden Thirteen went through?

Mr. Dille: There again, my memory is not as clear as I wish it were. I believe that I had a good deal to do with the indoctrination in terms of assuming the officer role in the Navy and anticipating some of the problems that would be faced, such as what happened the first time a black commissioned officer walks into an officers' club, or asks for a room at the BOQ, the bachelor officers' quarters—things of that kind. In terms of outward signs of military bearing, I think I had a good deal to do with that. Because I had so much military training of my own, probably a better kind than the Naval Academy did as far as physical bearing, proper posture, marching, saluting, and military courtesy, that kind of thing.

Paul Stillwell: In the integration of baseball there are stories about Branch Rickey counseling Jackie Robinson to turn the other cheek if necessary.[*] Was that the kind of advice you gave to these officer candidates?

Mr. Dille: I think in general there was that category, yes. I think that was anticipated. After all, these were all highly educated men who had played roles in their own private lives in dealing with problems.

Paul Stillwell: One interesting phenomenon I've observed is a difference in perceptions on how the instructors treated them. George Cooper, for example, feels that the

---

[*] Branch Rickey, the president of the Brooklyn Dodgers, in the fall of 1945 signed Jack Roosevelt Robinson, a black Army officer with a spectacular background as an athlete, to a professional baseball contract. In 1947 Robinson became the first black major league baseball player and endured a great deal of verbal abuse as a result; Rickey directed him to endure the abuse silently.

instructors were condescending. They acted as if they weren't really sure that these black men were up to grasping the material presented during their training as officers. Frank Sublett remembers nothing of that sort. I think it's partly a matter of their personalities and interesting that they would have those differing memories of their perceptions of that long ago.

Mr. Dille: Well, individuals have different sensitivities. The mind will attach different significance to different actions. Some individuals will be able to look over their shoulders and walk away from it. Others will record it as a [unclear].

Paul Stillwell: Another interesting difference was in the degree of pressure they apparently felt. Some believed that they were representing 8,000-10,000 men apiece—whatever the number of black enlisted men in the Navy at the time. And others felt they were just doing it as individuals. Did you observe them to be under a good deal of pressure in this environment?

Mr. Dille: You're going to have to explain that framework once more.

Paul Stillwell: All right. Some felt that they were representing large numbers of black enlisted men. Whatever they might achieve, it was not just an individual failure or success; it was a failure or success on behalf of the race. Others just went through it as individuals rather than taking that burden on themselves. Did you feel they were under a good deal of pressure?

Mr. Dille: Oh, I think there had to be pressure. We were instructing individuals who differed in their reactions and their attitudes. But it would seem to me there was a pretty uniform feeling that they were torchbearers; they were standard bearers. It was important that they succeed, not for their individual glory alone but for what they represented.

Paul Stillwell: Another phenomenon I've observed is that they didn't seem to be from a common mold, except in their leadership attributes. They came from a variety of colleges. Some had graduate degrees; some had bachelor's degrees; some had partially completed college. And I'm guessing that the Navy did that deliberately as a test to see how different individuals would react. They could easily have all master's degrees, for example. But that probably wouldn't have been as legitimate a test as to have the variety.

Mr. Dille: Well, of course, I have no real knowledge of the Navy's discussions or adoption of a philosophy in selection. My impression was the Navy simply put out the word throughout the entire Navy to submit names of outstanding black individuals; I doubt if they discussed initially what it was for. They said essentially, "Send us the biographical background on them, and we'll make a choice from that." I think they all had college degrees.

Paul Stillwell: Not all of them. For example, Arbor didn't. Sublett didn't.

Mr. Dille: Well, that surprises me. They must have had outstanding records.

Paul Stillwell: I think it was based on the leadership that they demonstrated in the enlisted setting. And I think that this was also the difference between 1942, when you were seeking a letter from Dr. Hutchins, and 1944. The requirement for a degree was not nearly so important two years later as it had been at the outset of the war.

Mr. Dille: Maybe the formality they recognized wasn't significant enough to indicate [unclear section]. Dalton Baugh, Sylvester White. I'm sure it came from family background and education that was pretty sophisticated. They were from a more metropolitan, sophisticated background. At the other extreme was Graham Martin, who was a graduate of the University of Indiana and a great tackle on the football team. I remember that. He came from a little town whose name is almost comical.

Paul Stillwell: Tobacco Port.

Mr. Dille: Yes, Tobacco Port, Tennessee. There was one other from a little town.

Paul Stillwell: Well, the achievements of these men in later life were a testimonial to what capable people were picked to go through the program.

Mr. Dille: [Unclear section]. And, of course, we've lost a few, including Dennis Nelson. He was very sharp.

Paul Stillwell: What recollections do you have of him from 1944?

Mr. Dille: Oh, none that I would try to express as distinguishing him from the others or even try to go down the line of the others. Again, I'd be leaning on memory, and that might be overcast by my more recent contacts with them. Because I have been in contact with them all these years. I've been to as many of their reunions as I've been able to. They've been kind enough to invite me, and I have joined them.

Paul Stillwell: Well, that feeling is reciprocated, because they're grateful to you for your continuing interest and support.

Mr. Dille: I will be there as long as I'm physically able. And then, of course, I've been trying to get a ship named for them.

Paul Stillwell: What came of that effort? How did you proceed on that?

Mr. Dille: Well, for some years I went through discouraging experiences. My primary contact was the Secretary of the Navy, feeling that since he was a civilian he would, hopefully, be more sensitive to the public relations aspect, the import of recognizing this kind of thing.

I knew from the outset that naming a ship would be difficult, because, as most of us know, aircraft carriers are largely named for battles, and battleships are named for states, and cruisers are named for cities, and submarines, I believe, are named largely for fish. So there's really not a category of important ship that I could single out to shoot for.

But I thought there might be a transport, for example, that might be suitable. And I had a couple of other things.

It took a while to get the letter, really, to the Secretary's attention. Of course, it obviously would be screened, and for several years it came to a stop before it really got to the Secretary. Then I'd get a letter back, for example, from an admiral, or a rear admiral who was a staff man in the Secretary's office, saying, of all things, "The Navy does not discriminate in terms of naming ships, and therefore we cannot discriminate in favor of a special group." I thought that was about as awkward a phrasing as a man in his position could possibly come up with. Maybe he ought to be transferred to something else.

But given time, I wound up getting through to the Secretary, John Lehman.[*] Apparently the staff man who read the idea passed it on up to him, saying, "This probably deserves consideration, Mr. Secretary." And he suggested that there was a building that could be named for the group. I've forgotten what station it was.

The Secretary came right back in a memo to that man and said, "You're right. It should be recognized. It is important, but I want something bigger than the building you've named. How about that planned recruit training center at Great Lakes?" And that is a magnificent building, very substantial. So that finally took effect, and we had the dedication.[†] I have a letter framed and on my wall there, a very gracious letter and a very significant one, I think, from Admiral Trost, who was Chief of Naval Operations at that point. He refers to the Golden Thirteen and so on. So that was the culmination of a lot of hard work and effort, but very gratifying in the end.

Paul Stillwell: What are your memories of the occasion itself?

Mr. Dille: Well, I believe that was the period when I was having a great deal of trouble with the knee, and I was virtually a cripple. But I got there to Great Lakes. The largest single impression made on me was the fact that the commanding officer of Great Lakes

---

[*] John F. Lehman Jr., served as Secretary of the Navy from 5 February 1981 to 10 April 1987.
[†] The dedication took place on 5 June 1987 at the Great Lakes Naval Training Center. That was a most appropriate location because it was the site of the officer training for the Golden Thirteen 43 years earlier.

Naval Training Center was a woman, Admiral Hazard.* And I might add that she was a very attractive woman, the uniform aside. But a female admiral was something I'd not anticipated.

The event was significant. I've forgotten how many of the Golden Thirteen were able to be there, the survivors.† George Cooper and Sam Barnes both spoke for the Golden Thirteen. And it was a very happy occasion. In the lobby is a significant memorial, too, to the Golden Thirteen. So we finally made it on that project.

Paul Stillwell: One thing that the men of the group have told me is that they were handed their commissions individually, privately. There was no graduation ceremony per se. But I suggested to Dr. Barnes that essentially this building naming and that celebration amounted to their graduation ceremony, 43 years after the fact.

Mr. Dille: Well, I suppose it could be viewed that way, although I don't think it was a matter of the Navy trying to make up for anything. They just recognized the symbolism and significance of the Golden Thirteen, and what they had accomplished.

Paul Stillwell: Were you gone from Great Lakes by the time they got their commissions?

Mr. Dille: I believe so. I have no memory of being there at the completion of their schooling.‡

Paul Stillwell: I talked to Lewis Williams last year, known as Mummy. He was one of the three of the original 16 who was not commissioned. He recalls you telling him that the reason he was not commissioned was because of his involvement as a labor organizer on behalf of railroad station redcaps. I gather you have no recollection of such a conversation.§

---

* Rear Admiral Roberta L. Hazard, USN, Commander Great Lakes Naval Training Center, July 1985-July 1987.
† All eight members of the group still alive in 1987 attended: Arbor, Barnes, Cooper, Hair, Martin, Reagan, Sublett, and White.
‡ The members of the Golden Thirteen received their commissions in mid-March 1944.
§ The interviewer and Mr. Dille discussed this subject prior to the beginning of the tape recording.

Mr. Dille: I certainly do not have any recollection of that in trying to think about it, nor can I think of what my source of information might have been.

Paul Stillwell: Well, all of the members of the group were investigated by the FBI. Did you have access to those FBI reports?

Mr. Dille: Not to my recollection. It's possible that if I'd asked for them, I might have had access to them, but I do not remember studying them.

Paul Stillwell: But you certainly don't remember that as being a disqualifying factor.

Mr. Dille: No, I do not.

Paul Stillwell: Do you have any knowledge of why the three were not commissioned?

Mr. Dille: No, I can only assume that either the Navy felt that the 12, and the warrant officer, completed their designated project, and that the others were supernumerary, or perhaps that their ranking and their performance were not as high as the others.[*]

Paul Stillwell: I have yet to find any official records that really explain that. I hope I can.

Mr. Dille: I would think that the best source, of course, would be the Navy. But whether they kept accurate records, I don't know. I have no idea whether that's the kind of record they would keep in normal filing.

Paul Stillwell: I don't either.

---

[*] Bernard C. Nalty, *Strength for the Fight* (New York: The Free Press, 1986), makes the following statement on page 192: ". . . on January 1, 1944, sixteen black enlisted men entered a segregated officer candidate school at the Great Lakes Naval Training Station. Although all of them successfully completed the course, only twelve received commissions, a purely arbitrary number adopted by the Bureau of Personnel for reasons never explained. Of the remaining four, one became a warrant officer, and the others reverted to enlisted status."

Do you have any other recollections or highlights of your reunion meetings with the group over the last dozen years?

Mr. Dille: No, nothing other than generalizations such as my wife going with me to some of them. Frankly, I have been very pleasantly surprised at how compatible she was with the wives of the Golden Thirteen, and how much they had in common, how much they had to talk about. Because, of course, she grew up on the south side of Chicago, and was a graduate of the University of Chicago, as I was. And she went to private school for the most part. She really has never had much exposure or contact, so it was an interesting thing for me to observe.

Paul Stillwell: Do you have any overall concluding observations on your relationship with the group?

Mr. Dille: I think only that I feel I learned a great deal. I guess all of my life—my activities, my major interests, and my business career—has been what I would call people-oriented. So I've always been interested in people and how they conduct themselves, how they react to different things, different situations, and what are their standards of courtesy, conduct, expressions of affection, things of that kind, expressions of warmth. These men I've always thought were pure gold. Oh, I could think of things that I could have said about them, just as they could have about me. But I feel I learned a great deal from them, and still am learning from them when we get a chance to get together. And we talk on the phone once in a while. I've talked to George Cooper and Sam Barnes a couple of times.

Paul Stillwell: What sorts of things have you learned from them?

Mr. Dille: Well, perhaps I would not have used the word "learning" in terms of acquisition of academic knowledge or things of that kind, but the observing how they react to different subjects. Whether it be the resistance I ran into trying to get a ship named for them, or whether it be a more generalized subject like the events that take place now and then about racial relationships that come up in the news, various things of that kind.

We'll exchange ideas. I ask them what they think, and I learn something from that, and I am somewhat guided myself in terms of any relationship I may have to editorial policy for my publications. I've had an opportunity to talk about more intimate things that you wouldn't be able to talk to just a casual acquaintance.

I remember, for example, having lunch with Judge White, Sylvester White, one day. Among other things, I asked him what difference, if any, the degree of skin color makes among the blacks themselves. Are you a whole lot better off within your own community to be very light skinned, or are you better off, really, to be more of an original and be of a very dark skin? He didn't feel it made a significant amount of difference. But that is only an example of the kinds of things you can talk about if you're good friends and learning things that way.

Paul Stillwell: That brings me the end of my questions. I'm grateful for the opportunity to talk again.

Mr. Dille: Well, I appreciate your coming, and it's a fascinating subject to me. I'm glad to participate any way I can be helpful. If there's anything you want to discuss in terms of revision, we can do it by phone. I'll be available at any time, because this has been an important experience in my life.

Paul Stillwell: Again, thank you very much.

Launched in 1969, the U.S. Naval Institute's award-winning oral history program is among the oldest in the country. Used in combination with documentary sources, oral histories offer a richer understanding of naval history through candid recollections and explanations rarely entered into contemporary records. In addition, they help depict the atmosphere of a particular event or era in a manner not available in official documents.

The nonprofit Naval Institute accomplishes its history projects through contributed funds and gratefully accepts tax-deductible gifts of all sizes for this purpose. This support allows the Institute to preserve the life experiences of today's service men and women so they may enlighten and inspire future generations.

For information about opportunities to underwrite Naval Institute oral history projects, please contact the Naval Institute Foundation at 291 Wood Road, Annapolis, Maryland 21402; by phone at (410) 295-1054; or by e-mail at foundation@usni.org.

Index to the Oral History of
Mr. John F. Dille Jr.

Arbor, Jesse W.
   Member of the Golden Thirteen, the first black naval officers, trained at Great Lakes Naval Training Station in 1944, 29-30, 52

Armstrong, Captain Daniel W., USNR (USNA, 1915)
   Served as officer in charge of Camp Robert Smalls for black sailors at Great Lakes Naval Training Station in World War II, 12-15, 20-21, 41-42, 47-49

Barnes, Phillip G.
   Member of the Golden Thirteen, the first black naval officers, trained at Great Lakes Naval Training Station in 1944, 30

Barnes, Samuel E.
   Member of the Golden Thirteen, the first black naval officers, trained at Great Lakes Naval Training Station in 1944, 30, 55, 57

Baugh, Dalton L.
   Member of the Golden Thirteen, the first black naval officers, trained at Great Lakes Naval Training Station in 1944, 30

Camp Robert Smalls
   Site of recruit training for black sailors in World War II, 8-21, 41-45
   Site of training for the first black officers in 1944, 21-39, 45-53, 55-56

Cooper, George C.
   Member of the Golden Thirteen, the first black naval officers, trained at Great Lakes Naval Training Station in 1944, 31, 50-51, 55, 57

Dille, John F. Jr.
   Parents, 2, 4, 46
   Wife Jayne, 1, 31, 57
   Son John III, 1-3
   Civilian background before entering the Naval Reserve in 1942, 1-3, 40-41, 46-47
   Service at the Great Lakes Naval Training Station 1942-44, 3-35, 41-53, 55-56
   In 1944 commanded an ordnance battalion at Waikele Gulch, Hawaii, 27
   In 1945 was a Navy public information officer on the staff of Commander Service Force Pacific Fleet, 27, 35-38
   Connection with the Golden Thirteen in the 1980s, 53-54, 57-58

Discipline
   Problems at the Great Lakes Naval Training Station during World War II, 16-17, 41

Enlisted Personnel
    Recruit training at Great Lakes Naval Training Station during World War II, 3-21, 41-45
    A group of black enlisted men went through officer training at the Great Lakes Naval Training Station in 1944, 21-35, 45-53, 55-56
    In 1945 Dille was on the staff of Commander Service Force Pacific Fleet to publicize the achievements of black sailors, 27, 35-38

Golden Thirteen
    Group of black enlisted men who went through officer training at the Great Lakes Naval Training Station in 1944, 21-35, 45-53, 55-56
    Reunions over the years, 57-58
    In 1987 a building at the Great Lakes Naval Training Center was named in honor of the group, 53-55

Goodwin, Reginald E.
    Member of the Golden Thirteen, the first black naval officers, trained at Great Lakes Naval Training Station in 1944, 23-24, 31

Gravely, Vice Admiral Samuel L. Jr., USN (Ret.)
    The U.S. Navy's first black flag officer, commissioned in 1944, 22-23

Great Lakes, Illinois, Naval Training Station/Center
    Site of recruit training during World War II, 3-21, 41-45
    Training of the first group of black naval officers, the Golden Thirteen, at Great Lakes in 1944, 21-35, 45-53, 55-56
    In 1987 a building at the training center was named in honor of the Golden Thirteen, 53-55

Hair, James E.
    Member of the Golden Thirteen, the first black naval officers, trained at Great Lakes Naval Training Station in 1944, 31-32

Hazard, Rear Admiral Roberta L., USN
    As Commander Great Lakes Naval Training Center, presided at the 1987 dedication of a building to honor the Golden Thirteen, 54-55

Lear, Charles B.
    Member of the Golden Thirteen, the first black naval officers, trained at Great Lakes Naval Training Station in 1944, 32

Leave and Liberty
    For black recruits during boot camp at the Great Lakes Naval Training Station in World War II, 16

Lehman, John F. Jr.
While he was Secretary of the Navy in the 1980s, a proposal was approved to name a building at the Great Lakes Naval Training Center in honor of the Golden Thirteen, 54

Martin, Graham E.
Member of the Golden Thirteen, the first black naval officers, trained at Great Lakes Naval Training Station in 1944, 32-33, 52

McMorris, Vice Admiral Charles H., USN (USNA, 1912)
As chief of staff to Commander in Chief Pacific Fleet in 1945, did not appreciate the significance of a request concerning black newspaper reporters, 36-37

Nelson, Lieutenant Commander Dennis D. II, USN (Ret.)
Member of the Golden Thirteen, the first black naval officers, trained at Great Lakes Naval Training Station in 1944, 29, 33, 53

News Media
Dille's work in newspapers and radio before and after World War II service in the Naval Reserve, 1-3
Coverage of Navy recruit training in World War II by *The Chicago Defender*, 7-8
Coverage of the achievements of black sailors in the Pacific in 1945, 36-37

Public Affairs
In 1945 Dille was on the staff of Commander Service Force Pacific Fleet to publicize the achievements of black sailors, 27, 35-37

Racial Issues
Segregated training for black sailors at Great Lakes Naval Training Station in World War II, 8-21, 41-45
Training of the first group of black naval officers, the Golden Thirteen, at Great Lakes in 1944, 21-35, 45-53, 55-56

Reagan, John W.
Member of the Golden Thirteen, the first black naval officers, trained at Great Lakes Naval Training Station in 1944, 33

Richmond, Lieutenant (junior grade) Paul D., USNR (USNA, 1942)
In 1944 devised the curriculum for the training of the first black naval officers at Great Lakes Naval Training Station, 24, 49-50

Service Force, Pacific Fleet
In 1945 Dille was on the staff to publicize the achievements of black sailors, 27, 35-38

Sublett, Frank E. Jr.
    Member of the Golden Thirteen, the first black naval officers, trained at Great Lakes Naval Training Station in 1944, 33, 52

Training
    Recruit training at Great Lakes Naval Training Station during World War II, 3-21, 41-45
    Training of the first group of black naval officers, the Golden Thirteen, at Great Lakes in 1944, 21-35, 45-53, 55-56

Trost, Admiral Carlisle A. H., USN (USNA, 1953)
    While he was Chief of Naval Operations in the 1980s, a proposal was approved to name a building at the Great Lakes Naval Training Center in honor of the Golden Thirteen, 54

Turek, Commander William, USNR (USNA, 1926)
    During World War II commanded the recruit training organization at the Great Lakes Naval Training Station, 13

Van Ness, Lieutenant Donald O., USNR (USNA, 1935)
    Was involved in training black recruits at the Great Lakes Naval Training Station during World War II, 13, 49-50

White, William Sylvester
    Member of the Golden Thirteen, the first black naval officers, trained at Great Lakes Naval Training Station in 1944, 22-24, 28, 33-34, 58

Williams, Lewis Reginald
    Black sailor who went through officer training in 1944 but was not commissioned, 23-24, 55-56

www.ingramcontent.com/pod-product-compliance
Lightning Source LLC
Chambersburg PA
CBHW080610170426
43209CB00007B/1385